Not Long Before The Morning Light
. . . and in time for the celebration of
The True Light

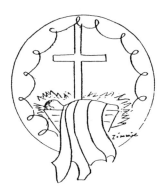

. . . A collection of Christmas memories
by
Zimmie Goings

"Not Long Before The Morning Light"

ISBN #0-9717166-0-9 (softback)
Copyright © 2001
Zimmie R. Goings
oftentimes called "Zim"

Residing in Alexandria, Virginia

Orders to:
Ragged Robin Books
P.O. Box 30213
Alexandria, Virginia 22310-0213

Printed in the U.S.A. by
BookMasters, Inc.
2541 Ashland Road
Mansfield, Ohio 44905

Illustrations and photographs are
Property of the Author.

<u>Acknowledgements</u>

Biblical references included in these letters
are from The King James translation.

Dedication

These thoughts. . . and these words
of Christmas memory
are lovingly dedicated to my children
Ronnie and Jon . . .
To my grandchildren
Christopher. . . Jesse . . . and Zachary
To Allison. . .
To my fine-furred friends
Maggie (in Kitty Heaven), Katie (beneath the
powder room vanity) and Midge. . .
the newcomer to the Christmas tree. . .

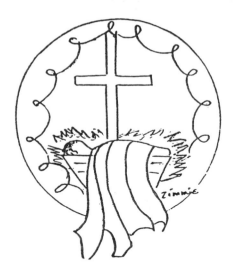

to my extended family of friends
who will surely find themselves
somewhere among the pages. . .

and especially to The Christ Child. . .
the Giver of Light!

Foreword

As Christmases come and go I find that all sorts of happenings in our lives come together to tell about how we look at Christmas. Though living in northern Virginia most of my adult life, I suppose real Christmas came to me first as a small child in a Methodist children's home in Macon, Georgia.

Many October mornings have come and gone since I stood on the porch of my grandmother's house. . . in the small town of Wrens, Georgia. . . up the road from the small shanty house where my parents lived. . . and waited to be taken somewhere else to live. There were other people there too. . . probably my grandmother and others in the family and the people who would take me away. I did not realize what was going on. It was 1942 and I know now that we were very poor. The conversation seemed to be about what time we would leave. . . and I seem to remember thinking even then that if we were going to go. . . then we should go.

I remember standing on that same front porch another morning before that. . . I don't know exactly when. . . but sometime in my fifth year. It was a sunny morning. . . with very blue skies. I remember that my mother was there. . . and she was going to go to the hospital. I remember looking at her shoes and wondering why one side of them was brown and the other was white. I didn't know about spectator shoes then. . . just that her shoes were peculiar and didn't seem to match. I also didn't know what "going to the hospital" meant. I didn't know that my mother was ill . . . I did not know that I would never know her again . . . and I never did know her again after I left that porch on a sunny morning . . . with blue skies. . . and went to live among a hundred or so other orphans and children from unhappy circumstances.

I don't remember the ride there. . . only that when I got there, there was a woman. . . a woman with dark hair. . . a pretty woman, I thought. A woman I wanted to believe was my mother. She wasn't, of course . . . but I suppose I had a longing for her to be. When later I would see my own six-year old grandson and his innocence and his small little person, I realized how small I was when all of these things happened to me and how frightened I may have been and how little understanding I had of the events in my young life. I'm not sure what, if anything, I brought with me.

I have no recollection of Christmas before then . . . but as one of a hundred or so children in the Children's Home I came to learn about true Christmas. I hold it preciously in my heart. Looking back at my Christmas letters as an older person. . . I can see that I have brought those early Christmas moments with me. . . of coming to a tree on Christmas morning . . . one which we had joyously decorated with all the pretty lights and tinsel . . . all but the icicles which someone older than we so perfectly put there one by one . . . where we'd be excited to get a shoe box filled with hard candies, nuts, a candy cane, perhaps a tangerine, perhaps a doll to play with or some special thing we longed for. We shopped for our friends with $2.00 of Christmas money in our pocket or tied in the corner of a handkerchief and had enough left over to buy a little something for ourselves. There was enough.

We played Mary and Joseph in chenille robes and towels and made angel wings with crinoline, tissue paper and glue.

I brought childhood Christmas to the lives of my children, and they into the lives of their own. They helped me to keep it in mine. My heart lets me know that Christmas is about sharing . . . and about the Christmas child and others. One cannot bypass Christmas. . . the true Christmas. . . and be wholly content.

Christmas means many things to me now -- The manger. . . and knowing that it and the cross are each a part of our hope. . . so intimately tied together just as the unending circle of the Christmas wreath . . . the bright lights of candles which represent the light of Christ. . . the choirs of angels and others . . . sharing. . . the generosity of spirit . . . the excitement of coming to the tree on Christmas morning. . . little presents that remind us of the Gift given us. . . the twinkle of eyes and the tender spirit that surrounds us. . . our children. . . their children. . . our friends . . . the knowledge that there is someone out there who may not have Christmas . . . but also someone out there to help them have it. . . and the confidence that Christmas will always come to us. . . if we wait for it . . . welcome it . . . believe in it . . . and continue to hold it dear.

. . . Christmas 1984

I think of each of you. . . specially. . . and hope that this letter which I ask you to share with one another will not lack personal touch or the warmth which I attach to each of our relationships.

We go from Christmas to Christmas, it seems, as if turning but one calendar page, and yet those pages in between bring us to another Christmas card and a sharing of another year's moments.

This passing year has seen good friends go off in different directions. . . some too far away to see . . . others just out of reach in our daily travels. . . children continue to grow and move out in their own directions. . . new interests in my life. . . I feel a continuing personal growth and awareness. . . and it's good.

Last Christmas's costuming of "Amahl and the Night Visitors" for our church paved the way to become involved in costuming for Springfield Community Theatre's production of "Joseph and His Amazing Technicolor Dreamcoat" in the Spring. I was invited to work with "Sound of Music" but there were timing conflicts. Dancing in "Amahl" last Christmas brought me to choreograph the dance for this year's "Carols In the Round" which we'll share with our church members and friends in a Christmas tableside setting Sunday evening.

It is what we've come to call a "Folk Waltz" danced to an old English carol ("Tomorrow Will Be My Dancing Day")... the girls (and I use that word lightly) dressed in bright red and green taffeta Christmas tartan plaid skirts, ruffled blouses and black satin weskits trimmed with green, gold metallic and white lace edging. The guys will wear dark trousers with cummerbunds to match our skirts, dressy shirts -- and there will be sprigs of holly and berries to adorn our hair and the guys' shirts. The costuming is mostly mine... and I love it... I have missed my calling... and simple though these pursuits be ... they're creative, colorful and fulfilling.

Springtime brought the announcement of my son Ronnie's wedding plans... and I enjoyed creating his bride's wedding gown and veil (and my gown, too) ... planning the wedding ceremony (in particular the music) for them and designing the program that will remind them another day of the sweetness of their special moment. And so, as this year has brought me a lovely daughter to share my son's life... surely the years to come will bring happy announcements of new and special little people to love... and I wish that for them.

Jon has spent the last many months living and working in Ocean City, Maryland, and though I miss him, it is a part of nature's plan that our children expand their horizons.... And as they expand theirs... so do I expand mine... but as regards <u>this</u> horizon it comes of necessity, not desire. These last ten years have caused me to wonder if it is gypsy blood that courses through my veins. Condominium conversion causes me to go in search of a new place to "hitch my wagon" in the next three months . . . I must convince myself that it is an <u>adventure.</u> . . or at least only a temporary inconvenience.

Early October allowed a lovely time on St. Simons Island with a Scottish friend. . . who came to love the Island too. . . though perhaps not in the same way as I. . . for I knew it as a child and have kept it (often only tucked away in my heart) as my special place over the years. . . just as there's a place in the hills of North Georgia which I keep tucked away. . . and those who've known the spirit of St. Simons or that of Young Harris will understand. More than 25 years have kept some of us in touch. . . and there are friends who've come along in the years since. . . even in the last few months. . . here in Virginia and Washington . . . whom I've come to treasure. . . my faithful circle of friends here. Our friendships continue. I think of friendship and I think of one who calls faithfully to have breakfast on each Thursday morning . . . the friend who tramps around with me on Saturdays doing errands and just having fun. . . the ones who love antiquing as much as I. . . the friend who also loves theatre enough to share five of her busy evenings and, we, the high price of tickets, to enable us to enjoy a season of theatre. . . the friend who gave me Christmas in the form of a perfect tree. . . and the caring which made it more perfect. . . the friends who always say "I'll help you". . . my special Georgia people who keep a bit of Georgia reserved for me. . . the young people who choose to be my friends. . . and that is a compliment. . . those friends far away who continue to keep in touch when my letters are slow in coming . . . those people in my work life over the years who have taught me and encouraged me. . . remembered me in special ways. . . and blended our business lives with friendship. . . and I think of those who place their trust in me when they need a friend.

My friends are scattered from Virginia to Georgia to California, to Colorado, to Texas, to Chicago, to Connecticut, to Maryland, to Mississippi, to Florida and there is one who travels abroad. . . and yet I feel I have them still. . . and that, along with the gift of my children, is the gift I count over and over again as precious. It needs no ribbon. . . no wrap. . . and can only be held in the heart. . . but isn't that the best way?

To each of you who has been my friend over these years. . . I love you and thank you. To each of you who has borne grief this year. . . I weep for you and offer you my hand. And to those who've known joy. . . I feel more joy for you. To one who may be lonely, I wish you a new friend and good company to keep. I wish us all good health and enough good fortune and I wish each and every one of you Christmas in your hearts and that peace which is born of real Christmas.

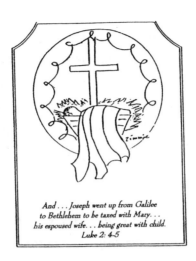

And . . . Joseph went up from Galilee
to Bethlehem to be taxed with Mary. . .
his espoused wife. . . being great with child.
Luke 2: 4-5

. . . Christmas Night 1985

*Christmas is just about past. . . and so this
becomes a reflection of it rather than a wish for it.*

*Christmas cards lie on the shelf still unaddressed
. . . and letters to friends not written. . . but would you
forgive me if you knew I was busy making clothes for the
Wisemen?*

*Lights on the Christmas tree still twinkle. . . and
it does give a wondrous message as the song tells us. . . and
the branches offer a new place to play for Maggie and
Katie, my little feline friends. Katie is a tabby cat and
the story goes that the "M" on the tabby's forehead stands
for "Madonna" or "Mary," for it was the tabby who
stayed close to the Infant Jesus and kept him warm.*

*The last bit of lace was placed in time on gifts
fashioned for special choir friends at Christmas Eve
Candlelight service last night. We processed to "The
Little Drummer Boy" and recessed by candlelight to "Joy
to the World." A small child was there uttering his own
little sounds. . . and we all know that a wee babe gave us
Christmas so long ago. . . only, this small child is my first
grandchild, and he, too, is a true gift to our lives this
Christmas. . . and he too is love.*

*The Holy Family had needed to be dressed for a
German Christmas program to be given by the*

Sanctuary and Children's Choirs Sunday night. . . Three Kings needed crowns and cloaks . . . and shepherds their drapes, and fifty or so choristers needed Bavarian skirts or bow-ties or suspenders to add color to Bach and Handel. Three shepherds turned into four, three kings into two. . . and the third and finest crown was last seen traveling East. The shepherds. . . some of them. . . ended up with drapes inside out, one with a safety-pin adorning his forehead, and Mary's hair was so clean, her shawl would not be stayed. . . and the Infant was a Cabbage Patch doll. . . but this little Mary loved him too.

I have been pleased to costume our choir these last three years, and to see a faint vision become a lovely reality has been a joy. Sewing the final stitches, placing the last sequin on a gold crown and constructing bow ties until 2:30 in the morning for nights running puts sand in the eyes but a memory in the heart. It is lovely to set the imagination free to see what it fashions. . . it is my spirit at play.

As I reflect on Christmas, I reflect on the young people with whom I work and share fellowship in our Methodist youth group at church. There is something very special about being loved by young people and having them as your friends. It is genuine and unharnessed.

. . . continues

As I reflect on Christmas. . . I reflect on my friends who share their lives with me. . . who care . . . who often place their cares in my hands and trust me with them. I know not why. But I value it that they do. I value their faith in me and pray for something right to give back.

As I reflect on Christmas. . . I reflect on the gifts gathered by our church members to help flood victims. . . on the couple who, rather than give gifts to one another, would take that money and see that it is given to a couple in greater need, who would not have Christmas remembrances otherwise. . . .

I reflect on the more than 200 poinsettias placed on our church altar for Christmas out of love for others . . . I reflect on our Minister who told us about "Our Savior" on Christmas Eve. . . . My eye is caught by the flame in the fireplace. . . and I feel grateful for a new hearth and home of my own this year. . . and the warmth of the fire causes me to reflect on the family and friends who have come and been warmed by it this holiday season . . . who have brought gifts both tangible and intangible . . . an English music box which plays "Green Sleeves". . . a fine brass cat who sits by the fireplace and causes the fine-furred ones to wonder. . . the pine cones from Denver to kindle my fires. . . a lovely blanket to warm my lap. . . a sweater knit by a friend's mother far away in Scotland

. . . a "granny gown" from a young friend who has adopted me as her "resident mother". . . and the love and joy brought me by these special people.

I reflect on those who have "gone home" to celebrate with their families. . . I wish them safe journey . . . and to those who are sick or low in spirit, I wish comfort.

I reflect with a very warm heart on my own family . . . my boys now grown into men. . . gathered around me on Christmas Eve for supper and warm cider and sharing. One can pause for a long, long time when reflecting on her children and all that their years have brought. . . and all that we hope for in their futures. I am pleased with the people they've become.

And as a part of my Christmas reflection, I think of you, my friends. . . and of Christmases that have gone before. . . of times we've known together. I miss those of you who've made changes in your lives this year. . . and I welcome those new friends who bring joy already.

. . . continues

My Christmas wishes will be late. . . but my reflections are fresh and heartfelt. . . and as I reflect on the passing of this special time. ... I will also think on the days that lead us to another Christmas next year. . . and until then I wish you love, warmth, peace and joy.

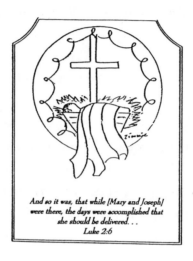

And so it was, that while [Mary and Joseph]
were there, the days were accomplished that
she should be delivered. . .
Luke 2:6

. . . Christmas 1986

"The Twelve Days of Christmas" keeps playing over and over in my head. . . and you know . . . the twelve days come <u>after</u> Christmas. . . and so those days and those gifts can be more easily focused on than those harried days that come before along with the dither of gift giving. I find that the closer one comes to Christmas. . . and the more moments one spends being with loved ones. . . the more carols one sings. . . the more giving of the heart one does . . . the more one feels Christmas. . . and the more one remembers where it all began. . . the better one can fashion a Christmas thought . For it is of the spirit.

But were I to write my own "Twelve Days of Christmas". . . one might find scattered there thoughts of

Three camels dancing. . .
Five songbooks singing. . .
Two cats in a Christmas tree. . .

and then I'd find a line to tell you about . . .

my small boy grandchild . . .
laughing and running. . .
loving and cunning. . .

about my two sons a-shining. . .
each in his own way. . .
and the lovely young ladies they cherish.

I'd tell of the good friends who're always there.
Then I'd try to find a way to relate those twelve days of
our Christmas to the twelve months of our year since last
we knew Christmas. . . to recall moments. . . for it is the
moments that count. . . experiences of the moment. . . those
special people who make the moments happen.

I'd recall for you my childhood as an "orphan kid"
when a local dime store would invite all of us from the
"children's home" to come and shop one early morning
before school, before the stores opened for business. . . and
we'd go in with our $2.00 and somehow we'd find a gift
for each of our friends and have something left over for
ourselves. . . and don't you find that it's true. . . that
when you share. . . you always have enough left over for
yourself? We were happy. Nowadays one goes with a
credit card and prays for will power.

I'd tell you about gifts that cannot be numbered
but definitely do count. . . like the sweet lady in our
church who is so sick. . . yet she would dedicate flowers on
the altar to someone else who she heard wasn't feeling
well. . . or the 92-year old Dutch lady who brings joy by
her mere presence and wonders why people are good to her
. . . or the friend who called the other evening to share a
kindness. . . not knowing I was having a sad moment. . .

or the little girl in my youth group who keeps saying "I'm sorry for not remembering your gift"... and yet her spirit... her verve... her young friendship and support are daily gifts... and I had to tell her so.

I'd tell you about a young friend who "claims" me as her "resident mother" who came and helped me put up my Christmas tree when her own heart was hurting over the death of her grandmother so close to Christmas... the friend who came and kept me company into the wee hours while I fashioned 60 cummerbunds for the Youth Choir to wear as they sang to our church about how "He Came In Love." I'd tell you about the joy I feel at having those youth in my life... to love and be loved by. We'll go to Chicago in the spring where they'll present another musical to a church there... and I'll be proud.

I'd write about the gift of "Celebrate Life" which our Youth Choir presented in the spring... the story in song of the life of Christ... and I was asked to design the camels. You know, those camels who carried the "We Three Kings of Orient Are"! They became life-sized... with long eyelashes... and sang and danced. Those camels and kings added a new dimension to my concept of the Christmas story ... but one would have to see to believe. And, after all — don't we earthlings ... most of us ... need to see in order to believe?

The children's choir performed "Kids' Praise"... a story about five larger-than-life Songbooks (which I enjoyed creating).   These books sang, played drums. . . even cried. . . and as we know, it takes more than a book cover. . . .   The books came to life . . . were brought to life by the characters inside.

*   I'd tell of four days at my small North Georgia mountain college, Young Harris, celebrating my 30ᵗʰ Class Reunion . . . bringing back memories of so long ago . . . hugging old friends. . . some not seen or heard from since Graduation Day. . . when we wrote in one another's books "I'll never forget you."*

*   I'd tell you about the good friends who've stayed close with me in heart over so many years. . . some so far away. . . of the friend who wants for a friend all the possible happiness and good that life can offer. . . understands moments of low ebb. . . and is glad in the high moments. . . of the friend who devotes time to tending animals for the humane society. . . out of love. . . and I think of . . . my two cats in the Christmas tree. . . my two little companions. . . Maggie and Katie. . . and there must be something in their stocking too on Christmas Eve. . . for they bring joy.*

*   I shall look forward to Christmas Eve when my family will gather with me. . . and we will share gifts from the tree, and from the heart . . . and the candles will be lit at Midnight Service and the choirs will sing . . . and we will remember the "First Day of Christmas". . . and the Gift.*

Good night. . . Merry Christmas. . . and a very blessed New Year.

And she brought forth her firstborn son,
and wrapped him in swaddling clothes,
and laid him in a manger; because
there was no room for them in the inn.
Luke 2:7

. . . Christmas 1987

I have thought a few times lately that "surely Santa Claus cannot stop at my house this year. . . as little thought as I've given to Santa Claus."

But, then, in contemplation, I realize how often the Giver of Greater Gifts has stopped here. . . and I see clearly how blessed I am.

I "fretted" to my pastor lately that I just had not "gotten the Christmas spirit yet". . . and that worried me. He said, "Well, 'Child' -- I just cannot understand why . . . as involved as you've been in all the Christmas activities at St. John's. . . you, of all people, should feel Christmas spirit." And I thought . . . yes, I feel as though I <u>have</u> <u>had</u> personal contact with the Christmas that happened so long ago. . . for I have been handmaiden. . . so to speak. . . to the Wisemen. . . tried to make humble the look of the shepherds. . . to lend humility. . . yet grace . . . and an aura of light to Mary and to blend Joseph's colors to those of hers to imply their unity. . . satin and lace "swaddling clothes" for The Baby to remind us that He was special. . . and a whole night and some more brought heavenly pink gossamer wings, edged in lace and ribbon, for the angels to wear. Yes. . . I felt in touch. . . but this body is weak from the late night labors. Perhaps the spirit sometimes suffers a bit too when the body tires!

This set the stage for the Youth Choir in our church to present "Birthday of a King" . . . with most of our traditional carols. . . and the walls of the sanctuary lined with banners bearing the names of those carols and designs by our Youth Choir Director depicting the carols and constructed over many sittings by five or six of us who love the youth. And then there were the candelabra lining the rows of pews. . . and the red ribbons. . . and the evergreen . . . and the whole wonder of that story!

I know that Great Giver stopped at my house, for He gave me the talent and the strength to fulfill my commitment to our Christmas story. . . and. . . "He got those angel wings done in time."

Earlier in December, our Sanctuary and Children's Choirs presented an International Christmas Festival. I was asked to coordinate costuming and decoration of the Sanctuary. Once more. . . so many visions came to my mind. . . ideas to share. . . and I saw them become realities in the performance. . . . I heard so many thank-you's and loving comments afterwards. . . this time last year my spirits were so low in my choral life . . . but something has happened. . . . A Gift! And I've been asked to be Chairman of Worship in our church next year (1988). People are enthusiastic and supportive of it. . . and I feel a real awakening happening among them.

The International Festival almost coincided with the Russian's visit here. . . and we devoted a segment of the program to Russia, using a tape by a minister who travels behind the Iron Curtain and "takes" Bibles there -- whatever way he can. Our offering that evening went to buy Bibles for him to take there. And then we had our 93-year old Dutch lady, Caroline, share her memories of Christmas in Holland. . . for we will not keep her for always. . . and she has much to share with us. We had Koreans. . . and a South African woman who sang a native song. It has been wonderful.

In the Spring, I traveled with our Youth Choir to Chicago where they presented the "LightShine" musical to a Methodist church and a nursing home (which touched the hearts of the youth). In spite of having to prepare for an emergency landing because the landing gear would not work properly, it was a delightful trip seeing the Windy City with those 60 or so teenagers and several adults. There were fearful ones among us, but those youth just could not have been spared to a plane crash -- they have too much to accomplish yet. Our trip offered an evening in Chinatown, a cruise on Lake Michigan through the locks of the Chicago River, many interesting exhibits and fun places in the Museum of Science and Industry, a shopping spree in the Water Place Tower Mall and on and on. It was an experience to take them to the Hard Rock Café, too, which they had petitioned us to. It is a greater experience to be a part of this group. . . and if you've been loved by teenagers like these. . . you've known love. I do.

I was pleased to have a visit in the Fall from one of my former MYF (Methodist Youth Fellowship) teenagers who was real special to me. . . . She writes now and then and lets me know what she's doing in Mississippi and it's always positive. . . . She hasn't forgotten the good moments we shared in our group or the things she learned there. . . <u>that</u> is a gift. . . to know you've given something to add to the fabric of a young life.

Some of our MYF kids went to visit our elderly Sunday evening and took them heart-shaped grapevine Christmas wreaths which they'd put together. I saw the gift of love. . . and from where does it come?

I will not elaborate on my work life this year other than to say we underwent a relocation to Pennsylvania Avenue, which, while the offices and views are lovely, has required of our patience and physical endurance. I pray for more of each.

I have to ask the forgiveness of all those whose birthdays came and went. . . and for the lack of communication since I sat here at this table <u>last</u> year and wrote you a Christmas letter. The year has been fast and the pace hectic. Please know that I think of you.

The year has seemed to have more than its share of sadness. . . with the death, among others, of Phyllis Huson who sang with us in the Choir and always was such an "up" person. . . two friends have had to deal with breast cancer. Grant that they will be well from it. Some friends have moved away. . . and I miss them.

I've spent lots of hours wallpapering my house . . . and I'm almost done. I'd hoped to finish by Christmas. . . but angel wings and other things came into the picture. Christmas will keep without all the walls being papered -- but what would Christmas be if there'd been no angels?

My 2-1/2 year old grandson, Chris, who calls himself "Tiffer," came Saturday evening, so his Mom and Dad could go to a Christmas gathering. He and I decorated my tree. . . and he helped my Christmas spirit along. He calls me "Mommer" . . . and we're real good friends! I sat him on my lap and tried to find words small enough and ideas simple enough to tell him about Baby Jesus and Christmas . . . and I told him that though Santa brings good things like toys and candy. . . that Jesus was the best present of all. . . that He was brought to us by God who also gives us the sun, the moon, and the stars and the flowers and the birds. . . and Mommies and Daddies (and "Mommer") too. And he sat with a little face full of wonder as though he really wanted to understand. . . and who can say he doesn't? Tiffer is a gift just as that other little boy was!!

I spent last evening at the Kennedy Center (as the guest of my employer and his family) hearing the Choral Arts Society sing "Christmas Music"... and I'll share Christmas dinner with them too... they're special... and their sharing is a gift.

My long-time friend, Marty, and I celebrated Christmas over dinner the other night, before she leaves to have Christmas with her family in New England. She's come face to face with cancer this year and is brave. I believe she's won!!

Tonight brought four "old friends" (Sandy, Eileen, Inez and Edie) to my house to enjoy Christmas and one another. We reminisced about the last ten or more years... ate a lot... laughed a lot.... We enjoyed our Santa-brought gifts and that other Greater Gift... Friendship.

Tomorrow evening my handsome sons, Ronnie and Jon, and their Ladies, Pam and Allison, and little Tiffer will come for Christmas Eve Dinner and gift exchange... a new realization of our love for one another ... and there will be Candle Light Service at the church ... and "Silent Night" will be sung into the early hour of morning....

And it will be Christmas... and Santa Claus will have come... and the Giver of Greater Gifts too

. . . and His Son. . . . And don't they really come from the same spirit. . . if we see them through right eyes? I believe so. . . it's the way it should be.

I think of you all and wish you warm Christmas love as I feel now. I will share that with my little feline family. . . Maggie and Katie. . . who offer me company and good humor each day. I count them among my blessings.

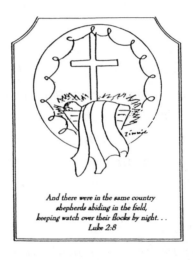

And there were in the same country
shepherds abiding in the field,
keeping watch over their flocks by night. . .
Luke 2:8

Excerpts . . . Christmas 1988

. . . *My eyes travel to my Christmas tree which shines with ornaments and memories of my family and friends who've shared my tree from year to year. I have from time to time called this my "friendship tree" remembering a year when life was hard and friends asked "what would you like for Christmas" and I answered . . . "just bring me an ornament from your tree." And they did.*

I notice there are unopened gifts there under the tree. . . some from some of my church youth who've affected my life. . . and I theirs. . . one from their choir directors Larry and Linda who have faith in me to help them make some magic in their performances. . . and yet we know who empowers us . . . who warms our hearts. . . who directs one's hands to create beauty. . . who helps us to know that <u>we</u> <u>can</u> if we believe.

There is a gift from my friend, Gussie, whom I've known for over 30 years now and her family too. She is strong and courageous. . . has endured serious back surgery this year and yet had the endurance and the love of a son to help her see Hawaii. There's one from a friend . . . a dear Scottish friend. . . who has found her content in Connecticut this year. . . and one from the attorney for whom I've worked over ten years now and I treasure all he is and stands for and his family too.

I look at my tree now and Maggie and Katie are relaxing around it. . . still in awe at why a tree that they should be able to climb has little lights that blink on and off. . . and little people and animals and birds and things that don't communicate . . . and angels with wings. Do you think there are angels in "cat heaven"?

I turn again to my tree and my eye is caught by the animated little people (dolls) who have eyes that open and shut. . . candles in their hands that they move back and forth. . . and I think there's something magical and special about dolls and dollmakers just as there is about children . . . and their Maker. I see a Christmas Bear whose paw waits to be squeezed so he can play Christmas songs to my 3-1/2 year old grandchild Chris, who will be here in all his Christmas excitement tomorrow afternoon with Ronnie and Pam to enjoy Christmas. His new word is "beautiful". . . and Christmas is! Ronnie and Pam continue to work hard to provide a good home . . . young couples do have to these days. They're good people and lovely parents.

My other son, Jon, took a very lovely bride in October. . . a _very lovely bride, indeed_ . . . and the wedding was a thing of beauty. Of course, I pray for their happiness and for their good fortune too. A very special lady I worked for when the boys were babies came to the wedding. . . and it was such an added treat to see her. Ethel, that's you!!

My year has been good, if exhausting. . . what with the pressures of a law firm. . . trying to contribute in the ways I can to help enhance the spiritual life at St. John's. . . trying to keep up friendships. . . family "good will" etc. . . and occasionally clean my house. Oh, dear!! And if Christmas wonders would not cease, lo and behold . . . I saw one convincingly real Santa atop an emergency vehicle last night when our Choir was out caroling. . . wishing Merry Christmas to all of North Springfield . . . and another caught in a window with both legs hanging out. . . will wonders never cease? I hope not!! I wish you and yours a lovely Christmas. . . a warm Christmas. . . and love to keep you through the New Year.

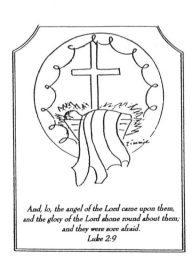

And, lo, the angel of the Lord came upon them,
and the glory of the Lord shone round about them;
and they were sore afraid.
Luke 2:9

. . . Christmas 1989

"On Forgetting Christmas"

*I cannot forget Christmas. . . nor must I forget
Christmas. . . nor must any of us forget Christmas
because Christmas is our assurance that life goes on. It is
our assurance that we are loved in a very special way.*

*I cannot forget Christmas when there is a small
child who says "I love you, Grandma". . . and I cannot
forget Christmas when I hear that same little boy saying,
"Grandma, couldn't you wait to decorate the tree? I
wanted to help you too." I cannot forget Christmas when
I look at a Christmas tree and think of the symbol of
friendship, and I think of each ornament on that tree
and it reminds me of somebody very special. . . reminds me
of a time shared together. Some remind me of times when
my children were littler boys and we sat around a table
and painted those ornaments that still hang on my tree.
And after painting, we'd bake gingerbread men and
hang them on the tree. . . and then maybe go shopping for
their little gifts.*

*I cannot forget Christmas when I hear the carols
sung by the children and the youth in the choirs in our
sanctuary at church. I cannot forget Christmas because
of the candles that glow or the little nativity that sits in
our narthex that this year was portrayed by porcelain
dolls in cotton clothing because the church was low on*

funds. . . . I remember a childhood friend who came to visit me this year after 30 years and I think about her and the Christmases we had in a children's home in Georgia and how when we were in Christmas plays we wore bathrobes and towels around our heads. . . but somehow I just couldn't seem to put bathrobes and towels around those porcelain dolls. . . and so I sewed "Jesus clothes" (as my grandson calls them) for them to wear. The cradle was made by some friends who furnished another cradle on the lawn beneath the cross, and whose babies had been rocked in it. There were children who came there to help me put the nativity together.

I cannot help but think about Christmas as I think back to a few days ago when my children were here and we shared Christmas together. . . and I remember Christmas, even though I have a child whose heart is breaking right now because his family is separated. . . because I have to know that he will find love again and that he will love this little child of his enough to make a difference. I know sorrow right now. . . but I know joy also. . . for I think of my other son and his young bride who will have a sweet little daughter in the Spring. . . and this is why I say that Christmas is our assurance that life goes on and love goes on. I've seen sadness this year and I've seen happiness. . . . I've seen death and I've seen birth. I've seen people who will be going away to Hawaii for three or four years. . . children of my friend of long ago. On Christmas Eve two of my special young married friends were at candlelight service . . . they had just flown in from Hawaii. Some come and some go. I think about the things I've seen on the news. . . the homeless being given clothing and the tears they shed for the joy of a warm coat. . . . I see the death and havoc in Panama. . . and yet I see other real signs of joy and love that people share with one another. I think about my friends in New England. One went there a while ago and now she's happy in her little country home . . . and involved in some light opera and little theatre and things like that and seems to enjoy "Mama Sheep" who lives close by with her lambs . . . and her other people friends.

I think of another friend who travels to New England each year to be with her family. . . and I miss her . . . but she was here today and we shared some hot drink and Christmas goodies together and reminisced about some old times and did some thinking about the New Year. My grandchild, Christopher, was here last night to help me celebrate New Year's Eve. He's fresh out of a case of Chicken Pox which he got for Christmas. We used to say "all I want for Christmas is my two front teeth," but he got chicken pox instead. In spite of that he was a lot of fun, and we played "Silly Dilly" this morning. . . a game I had not played before.

I expect some friends to drop by this evening . . . still to pick up a Christmas gift and it's January 1, 1990. . . and I feel a little bit guilty that my cards haven't gone out. Most of my gifts were given almost on time. . . and I saw a lot of special friends. . . and <u>those</u>

<u>cards still lie on the table.</u> . . but I think of each and everyone of you.

One part of my heart has said "Relax, ease up on yourself. . . send the cards later." But I thought, "No, I can't forget Christmas, because to forget Christmas is to forget that hope and that dream." Somehow I can't do that. Can you imagine how our lives would be if we had no Christmas? And I do wish that each of you had a special Christmas and a lot of love involved in it. I did the liturgy and helped serve communion for the youth service on Christmas Eve at church and it reminded me of six years ago when I joined this church on Christmas Eve and how excited I was. I wanted to run out and tell the whole world that I had found something special again. . . and that I had committed myself that night. . . given myself as a Christmas gift to the Christ Child and I wanted to share that this year with our young people. I wanted to share with them how special it is to be attached to a Savior. . . . There were some things I wanted to tell them. . . but not enough time to do it . . . . They sang their hearts out and then we all sang the "Silent Night" with a candlelight recessional. . . and it was beautiful. . . and when I came home that night. . . Midnight. . . Christmas Day now . . . I thought, "Oh, but the Christmas cards aren't done."

Somehow I still wasn't ready. . . when usually Christmas Eve is the night that I get my inspiration for those cards. And today after some friends had come and gone and my sweet grandchild, Chris, and my son, Ronnie, too, who is trying hard to be strong . . . somehow I thought about this thing of not writing Christmas cards and not seeing some people I might have made time for.

I thought back to some years ago when I was going through some trying times. . . when I thought "I really don't want to put up a Christmas tree" and then I thought, as now, "But I can't forget Christmas, and I must put up a tree for it's a sign of hope. . . a sign of life and a sign of joy. . . . It gives us the courage and it gives us the desire to go on into a New Year. . . reminds us of all the people who have been a part of our lives and the Christmases we've known. . . and it reminds us that Jesus loves us."

When I think about Jesus and how much he loves us. . . I still find myself thinking about some other friends I love. I think about a family down in a little town in southwestern Virginia called Konnarock many, many years ago when I was straight out of school and how they would invite all the friends of their children to spend Christmas or other holidays . . . sometimes three in a bed. As much space as there was to fill with people. . . they would invite that many more. They always spread a good table and had something special under the tree for everybody. They did so much . . . with so little. . . and I love them still. I remember caroling in the snows of Konnarock and how wonderful that was to me being a little Georgia girl and not having had much chance to *experience and enjoy the snow. I missed being with them this Christmas because the roads were icy and I was not feeling well. I missed being with them because they are a part of my Christmas. Even the years when I could not be with them... they were in my heart... and I remember something very special about them!*

I have some friends who go home to Pennsylvania every year and we had a little time together before they went this year.... They're friends of a long time. My Saturday Buddy has just worn herself out playing Mrs. Santa to all her friends... and there's a lady in Florida who I don't hear from much anymore... but she was there for me and my little boys when they were growing up. I hope that she's well. She's a very special lady.... There are other friends scattered around the countryside whom I think of. My young friend and "adopted daughter" was married in October. We put together a lovely wedding for her and Steve... and she has finally realized her long-awaited "marital bliss."

This year we had an exchange of ministers and I felt that when we lost that minister I kind of lost another special friend, but I guess friends don't go away in the heart or in the spirit.

There's a friend in Colorado who had a candle lit in my honor as part of their Hospice Center's 1989 Lights of Love. On account of the love she has for cancer patients and the work that she gives to the hospice centers, that light is special. If only I could bring to mind all the names of people who are special to me and could light lights for them. . . how bright a light that would be!

At any rate I just want to say how special Christmas is. . . and so are you. . . . Each Christmas let's remember one another and the bond of friendship . . . the bond of love. . . remember that Christmas is a covenant from God. . . of His promise. . . in that Baby Boy. . . called Jesus. He's loved us from the beginning of time and will love us for always. Cannot we give just a little of that to one another? A little belated Merry Christmas and a wonderfully happy New Year to each of you.

And now as I think about New Year's I realize that today I didn't get my bed made until well, well, well past Noon. . . . I couldn't get the cats out of it . . . isn't that something? They're God's creatures too. . . and in my manger scene I made sure to put a sleeping cat under the cradle. There's a legend that says it was the tabby cat who was the one who kept the little Jesus boy warm that night. . . and that's why the tabby wears an "M" on its forehead. It stands for "Mary." But surely I've told you that before.

Merry Christmas. God love you always.

Your friend.

And the angel said unto them,
"Fear not: for, behold, I bring you good
tidings of great joy, which shall be to all people."
Luke 2:10

. . . Christmas 1990

Somehow "the cradle and the cross" tells a very full story. . . the empty cross makes it complete. There is sweetness and sadness in each of our lives. . . . the cradle representing one and the cross in many ways the other.

This year has brought me the joy of a granddaughter named Jessica (Jesse) who was born . . . after a while. . . on April 30. She is a beautiful child and healthy. . . is doing all the normal things like cutting teeth and discovering the wonderful sound of laughter. . . and now and then the different sound of crying. Her Mom and Dad, Allison and Jon, are good parents and spend more time away from her at work than they'd like.

Ronnie continues to be a wonderful "Mr. Mom" and "Dad" to his son Chris. He works hard as a home and property appraiser and devotes most of his other time to Chris.

I continue to be busy at the law firm and as worship chairman in my church. The "busy" is good for me. There is fulfillment in my worship capacity because I have a chance to share the creative talents which God has shared with me. The church has looked so beautiful during Advent and will be during Christmas with its candles and wreaths and angels, and the sounds of Christmas from the choirs. Sometimes amidst the beauty

of the church there are struggles too . . . but one moves on.
Our youth directors resigned this year and that has left
me feeling quite empty and alone at times. We made
some magical moments together.

For various sad reasons I resigned my work as a
youth counselor. That, too, has left a hole in my heart. I
included as many children and youth as I could in
planning candle lightings for Advent and will continue
to try to hold them close spiritually. As in other years
friends have moved away and now and again new ones
come along.

Maggie and Katie look forward to my being at
home with them during the Christmas-New Year's week.
I promised them and me that we would sleep late
tomorrow. . . maybe light a fire and watch an old movie
. . . read a book. . . and by all means finish getting ready
for Christmas. God bless.

For unto you is born this day
in the city of David a Saviour,
who is Christ the Lord.
Luke 2:11

Christmas . . . 1991

I have searched and searched and find nothing that tells me that I wrote you at Christmas this year. . . perhaps it was one of those years when there was too much to do to find time to write. . . or too little to do to write an inspiring letter. I'm inclined to think it was not the latter. For I have lovely children and delightful grandchildren who certainly are ever present in my heart and mind. . . whether or not in my sights. . . I have a special ministry in my church. . . and as of December I resigned my position at Sutherland and went with my attorney to another law firm to take up there.

There is much that is similar from Christmas to Christmas. We re-celebrate the birth of the Baby Jesus. . . we sing carols and deck the halls. . . and parade the malls. . . and want so much for Christmas to be this very special time that warms our spirits and with the warming of the spirit the cold of winter is not so bad either. We tend to remember and hold close those we've always held close. . . our children and other family. . . and our extended family called "friends." We may write similar messages each year for there are those things we continue to find important. . . and sharings with those who are vital to our lives.

I find often that I send special store-bought Christmas cards to my family and perhaps do not always get around to sharing these types of letters. . . sometimes I *do and sometimes perhaps I just assume that they know about the highs and lows of my life . . . the excitements that perhaps they really don't see. Often I and others go to Hallmark and seek out those cards intended "for a special son " . . . or "for a special son and his family . . ." or "for a sweet grandson or granddaughter." We choose those to send. We want to know that we picked out something very special for them. Sometimes when I read the letters my sons write to me, I wonder if I shouldn't write more letters to them . . . heart messages. Hallmark may serve a purpose. . . but only we know the things that are in our hearts to say to our children.*

I will share with you a writing from St. John's newsletter, "The Chimes," which was preparatory to the coming of Christmas and an effort to share with the people in the church the different symbolisms in worship and how people all over celebrate The Important Birth of so long ago. I called it --

"The Lights of Christmas"

It was a long time ago in Bethlehem when that Boy Child Jesus was born on Christmas.

The time draws nigh that we celebrate again our Saviour's birth. We read again how the angel appeared to Mary. . . how a host of angels appeared to the shepherds and how the Kings followed a star . . . His Star. . . His Light. . . That Light for whom the world had waited so long. . . for whom it longs for a Second Time. We call it "Advent."

Advent brings with it a lighting of candles. . . a lighting of trees. . . a hopeful lighting of the heart . . . of the world's heart. Of even the most hopeless of hearts. It brings with it joy for the <u>most</u> of us. . . love for the <u>most</u> of us. . . peace for the most of <u>us</u> . . . it brings hope. . . hopefully. . . for all of us. For He is our very best Hope.

In our church as in others we celebrate Advent through the lighting of candles on an evergreen wreath. There can be three purple candles. . . one pink-colored and finally a white candle. . . the Christ candle of pure light. As we light the first purple candle, we think of the coming of Jesus. . . and we reflect on His second coming. As we light another purple candle, we think of John the Baptist who prepared the way for Christ. The rose- or pink- colored candle represents joy. The fourth candle. . . once again. . . purple. . . represents Mary who was chosen to bear the child of God in human form.

The color purple is a liturgical color used in churches and other places to denote royalty. . . for Christ is Our King. Some churches use the color blue to distinguish it from the Lenten purple and to represent anticipation of The Birth rather than the passion of Christ's death.

Candles have been used in Christian worship since the days of old to provide reading light. . . but also as a symbolism, signifying that Christ is the light of the world. He gives us spiritual light. . . shows us the way. . . does not let us fall.

We light many candles during this time. My first memory of candle lighting here at St. John's was the Christmas Eve I became a member of the church . . . and my heart remembered long into the night and into the days and years that followed the flames of the candles lighting other candles and the strains of the "Silent Night" finding their way out into the dark of Christmas Eve. . . the Light of Christmas. My heart was full as I and others sang that song over and over and over again until the church was emptied and filled with a dimmer light and that brighter light had gone out into the world to let people know that the Lord was born and the Light had indeed come. My heart still bursts a bit on Christmas Eve. . . and the light grows brighter. And I am made warm. I pray that you, too, are warmed by the Christ light.

And this shall be sign unto you;
Ye shall find the babe wrapped
in swaddling clothes, lying in a manger.
Luke 2:12

... *Christmas 1992*

Whenever I receive my first Christmas card each year, I am always excited to see who it's from, and I feel blessed that after so many years some of these friends still remember and send cards. I wish you each a wonderful Christmas and a new year filled with good health, prosperity, warmth and good people to love you.

In short, my year has been good in so many ways on account of the special people who cross my path, the fulfilling work that I do in worship in my church, the young friends there who look to me for friendship, laughter and sometimes a strong shoulder. I enjoy my work with the acolytes ("candle bearers") and continue to try to teach them how important their quiet ministry is and that to carry a light is to show themselves as Christians and as sharing their God-given talents. We are reminded to let our lights shine in a way that others may see our good [works] and glorify our Father in Heaven.

I enjoy watching my family as they raise their little children and feel pride as they work hard to succeed (and certainly success has many meanings other than the material or economic ones).

Chris played ankle-biter football this year and "hung tough," I hear. Ronnie is a wonderful father to Chris. Jon and Allison enjoy their little Jessica when they can catch up with her. She is indeed charming and melts my heart with her smile. They expect another little one in May.

The year has been good too because I've been able to see friends from earlier days and reach back in time to share sweet memories and bond again.

The church has been beautiful during this Advent time... if only my feet and body wouldn't get so tired during all the hours it takes to bring a magical Christmas look there. My mind and my imagination go wild... like a popcorn popper at times as ideas come to play in my mind. The acolyte celebration of lights on Sunday morning was inspiring and made my heart feel glad that I could design it in a way that seemed so like what our young people should present . . . what they might choose to say. Many called to say they were touched and shed a tear during the program. This is what life needs to be about -- to make a mark and to pass on the message of light and love.

There is little time to write... but I have enclosed a few of my reflections during 1992 which I hope you will enjoy. Love and joy to you.

P.S. Christmas is now past except for the nostalgia that goes with its passing. It was good. Christmas Eve thrills my heart. . . with the sweet story of The Birth. . . the excitement of those coming to church to honor it. . . to share gifts and signs of affection. I feel fortunate that my family is healthy and doing reasonably well in most ways and that I enjoy the gift of friendship with many and that I have my two little furry kitty friends, Maggie and Katie, to keep me company. Katie hid under the bed during most of Christmas Day when the grandchildren were here. . . and Maggie got into the catnip and first was quite happy and then quite disagreeable at his change of personality. No more catnip in our house, thank you!

Reflections of My Heart. . . Christmas 1992

"Advent"

Oh, come let us adore Him. . . Christ the Lord!

Advent begins soon. . . the time when we begin to celebrate anew the coming of our Lord Jesus Christ. What a beautiful word. . . the word Christmas. . . the mass of Christ.

It is a time when Christian hearts burn warmer
. . . candles shine brighter. . . perhaps we love one another
more. . . because we are reminded of how greatly we are
loved.

Often in worship my thoughts travel back in time
to other times and other ways in which we have celebrated
here this precious gift called Jesus. . . this sweet boy child
who came so many years ago. . . a wee earthling child. . .
but the Son of Almighty God . . . the Son of the young
Virgin maiden Mary. They say the stars shone brightly
that night. . . and especially one. They say the angels
sang and the Light shone all around.

This is the other light God Gave to us. . . after He
created the earth and gave us the sun, the moon and the
stars to guide us and give us light. He saw that His
human creation still needed a greater light and so He
sent us Jesus. . . to be a lamp unto our feet and unto our
souls. He knew that we still needed to be shown the way.
He gave us this special someone to travel our paths with
us.

And so at Christmas and other times we light
candles. . . symbolic of His presence in our lives and of His
love for us.

We light candles as evidence of His Word. He has
asked us to let our lights so shine that others may see our
good works and glorify our Father in Heaven. He has

taught us to carry our lights high and not hide them.
We need to share our special lights. . . talents we've been
given. . . in His name!

As Advent approaches, let us fill our hearts with
thoughts of our Jesus. . . the precious little earthling boy
who came to give us a good life. . . and to give us light in
our lives . . . to guide us. . . so long as we shall live.

*   *   *   *   *

"The Man in the Moon"

There was another time when I knew that the
lights of God call out to us to remind us of His love and
that of His son. I call it "The Man in the Moon." It was
one night before Christmas. . . when I worked late
putting up the Christmas tree for St. John's. . . I had
spent many hours with my son trying to locate a tree
stand. . . trying to cut the knots off the base of the tree so
it would fit. . . and hoisting this near perfect tree aloft to
stand tall and straight . . . this tree in our church to
honor the special birthday that comes during advent time
each year. . . the Birthday of our Lord! After putting
twinkling lights. . . like tiny stars. . . and tying over a
hundred red poinsettia blossoms on the tree. . . placing the
star on its top. . . enjoying time with my friend Fran who
came to help for a short while before she left to help
someone in crisis . . . feeling the twinge of fingers sore from
touching pine needles and holly. . . I started my journey

home. . . The tree was finished and beautiful I thought. . . but by then I needed someone else to think so too. Often God favors me (us) with a special star in His sky. . . a beautiful sunset. . . a sunrise. . . a rainbow. That night it was the moon with a very special glow around it. . . occasionally playing hide'n'seek with a cloud. There was a single star overhead. . . and The Man in the Moon seemed to smile. God seemed to be smiling from the moon. It was Christmas and I believe God knew that I wanted someone else to be excited about the lovely tree at the church and to care about these little things that I found myself happily doing sometimes in the late hours in celebration of His Christ Child. He smiled. . . while a single star shone overhead. . . and I hastened to tell a friend what I'd seen.

* * * * *

Toys in Heaven

This warmed my heart on another day. A little girl asked timidly but with a smile on her face "Will there be toys in Heaven?" One needs good answers for children, you know. I prayed quickly and hard for wisdom, "dear Lord, give me an answer for this child." I said to her "I can't believe in all my heart that there will not be toys in Heaven." And she smiled and asked one question after another similar to this. . . all about Heaven. I said to her that toys are special and fun, but there are also other things that make us happy and must be like a part of Heaven and she wanted to know what. I told her "love, like you feel with your family and friends . . . or your pet kitten or puppy; joy like you feel when something good happens to you. . . like your birthday party. . . happy memories. . . These things will last even longer than toys and never wear out." And she said, "Will I be like I am now in Heaven?" And I asked again, "Lord give me this answer too." And I asked her . . . "do you like surprises?" And her eyes lit up. "Oh, yes," she said. And I said, "We *don't know* exactly what Heaven will be like. . . but there will just have to be lots of surprises for us all, and it will be filled with love." We became friends. . . this little girl and I. One needs to seek the light of Christ in the heart to enlighten the small ones of His Kingdom. For they need honest answers, but hopeful ones. . . and after all, Christ said, "Of such is the Kingdom of Heaven." . . . as was He.

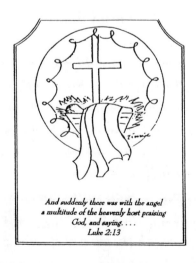

And suddenly there was with the angel
a multitude of the heavenly host praising
God, and saying. . . .
Luke 2:13

. . . Christmas 1993

How does one write of a whole year in those scattered moments granted at this time of year? A highlight of my year has been the birth of my third grandchild, Zachary, born of Jon and Allison, and who has a beautiful 3-1/2 year old sister Jessica (Jesse). My 8-year old grandson Christopher (Ronnie's child) was an important player on his little league football team, scoring several touchdowns and pulling any who would try to stop him along the field with him. He's tough but very gentle hearted. I'm proud of my sons, of course, that they're good people. That's success to me. . . good success.

A few good movies this year, some good Little Theatre, treasured reading moments (have you read "Bridges of Madison County"?). My work at the church, especially with the young people who light candles for worship, continues to give me joy and fulfillment, though I'm wrung out about this time each year. The tree at church is ready as are the banners and wreaths along the walls; my house will get its final trim when I stay home for Christmas week and hopefully have friends in and get an occasional catnap along with my kitty friends, Maggie and Katie.

Christmas Eve services will keep me up until past midnight but that's not sleep lost. . . but rather spirit gained.

No travel this year except to Atlanta, where there was an illness, but that afforded me a beautiful chance to get to know relatives whom I had not.

In February, if the Lord is willing, and I believe He will be, I will travel to The Holy Land with our minister Laughton and his wife Ruby and others, and will spend my birthday in Bethlehem. Can you think of a finer place to spend one's birthday than the birthplace of our Lord? It's a lifelong dream come true. One dreams of Bethlehem at Christmas. . . but February will be springtime in Bethlehem and that's His gift too.

I hope you're well, I hope you're happy, and I hope you are greatly blessed in your life and will receive your lifelong dreams if you haven't already. Judging from Christmas cards, I know that some of you have. I take joy in continuing to be remembered as part of your lives. Merry Christmas. . . with love.

. . . . continues

P.S. My Maggie Cat has found his place in the lap of the Christmas Teddy Bear to keep warm during Christmas and to wait for Santa, so all is well in various little parts of the world.

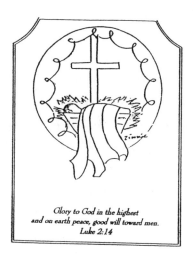

Glory to God in the highest
and on earth peace, good will toward men.
Luke 2:14

. . . Christmas 1994

Into each Christmas must come a child. . .
whether it be the original Christmas Child. . . the child
in each of us. . . our child . . . or our child's child. For it
was The Child who made for us this day called
Christmas.

It often appears that into each Christmas also
must come a cat. . . or two cats. Mine continue to love
Christmas. . . to believe the tree is put there just for them.
I had to laugh the other evening when I looked towards
my manger scene on the window sill and saw my Maggie
cat trying to find space within the stall to lie among the
little people and animals there. Mind you, the cat weighs
about 16 lbs., but he wanted to be in the midst of
Christmas. . . and perhaps to try to keep The Baby warm
. . . and himself. I found him later in a box which
contained a half-dozen cloth angel dolls. . . all nestled
warmly. And into each Christmas must come the angels.

It has been a special year for me. . . and I look
upon Christmas a bit differently this year. . . for I
traveled to The Holy Land in February to see the place
where Christmas began. It was a time of fear for people
there when there was a massacre in a temple -- over 20
people murdered while they prayed . . . close to 80 others
injured. There were soldiers with drawn rifles. . . and
people with stones. There was a couple who complained
that The Holy Land was not as they thought it would be

. . . perhaps they came hoping to find The Baby wrapped in a cloth and lying in a manger still. I don't know. But to think that after these 2,000 years people still pay homage to That Baby. . . homage enough that there are churches everywhere in His name. . . and people still come and fall on their knees to be closer. We rode the camels . . . walked on steps where Christ walked . . . walked among olive trees as He did. . . saw where He prayed . . . saw the caves around Jericho where the Dead Sea Scrolls were found by the shepherd boy. . . stood in the Jordan River for reaffirmation of our baptism as He stood there with John the Baptist. . . and more.

I brought a lot home inside me (and in addition about 300 pictures) and wrote a program about the life of Christ (looking through His mother's eyes) for the acolytes (candle lighters) in our church to welcome the Christmas season as they rededicated themselves. We made a tabletop display of Bethlehem, the Shepherds' Fields with blooming almond trees, Cana and the First Miracle, the River Jordan, and the City of Jerusalem, complete with lots and lots of little "Jesus people," a temple, camels, donkeys, fishes and loaves, etc. It was touching to the people who came to see and hear . . . and maybe most of all to me. . . I don't know. It was a gift I had to give back. One must go to those holy places to understand.

It's otherwise been a busy year -- my job in the law firm keeps me so very busy. . . but I guess that's good. I *continue to work in the worship area in my church and enjoy that.*

My grandchildren (Chris (9), Jessica (4) and Zachary (1-1/2)) continue to be beautiful and full of life. Chris quarterbacked for his boy's club league this fall and was tearful when the season was over. Ronnie (his dad) coached and derived a lot of satisfaction from working with the kids, as I do with those in my church. Jon and Allison and the other two little ones have moved to Front Royal recently to a lovely home there surrounded by mountains, and it's beautiful but seems so far away from me.

I will take the two weeks surrounding Christmas to be home and relax a bit, perhaps have Christmas suppers or what-have-you with friends and see my family on Christmas Eve and Christmas Day.

We've been busy making the church beautiful for Christmas, each week adding something more. It builds excitement among the people, and if we leave anything out, someone asks where it is. One of my friends who helps me with crafting things there, has threatened to hang me on the glass wall in the church, if she doesn't get her "great angels" made.

I have these visions around Christmas, you see, and I and others work to make them happen. One vision won't happen until 1995 because of the complexity of it.

But it _will_ happen. One day I hope to see a wrap-around tapestry on the back wall of our sanctuary, depicting the life of Christ. There is not enough time in this life. We have to use it well.

Life has been good to me, and I have stayed well. More people call me "M'am" these days, more people worry about my climbing on ladders and picking up heavy things. But they don't realize that I have lots of spirit and spirit helps to keep one strong. God holds my ladder and helps me with my load. I'm grateful to have you all out there to think about and to attach memories to. I am wishing each of you special blessings as you move closer towards Christmas and all that it brings. I hope that you are well, happy, warm, and enjoy good fellowship with those around you. And I wish you love.

P.S. Bella's "great angels" remind me of a Christmas Eve when Chris was with his Dad and me at church and in his little boy Christmas voice exclaimed, when the youth music director got up to direct the choir . . . and raised his white robed arms to instruct the singers to stand . . . "Grandma, grandma, the great white angels have come, grandma! The great white angels!" Out of the mouths of babes!

I'm reminded too of another time when a friend and I took Chris to the Mormon Tabernacle in Kensington to see the Festival of Christmas Lights where there was also a silent nativity "going on." Chris bundled in a cap too large (mine) and gloves too large (my friend's) stood just at stage edge with his chin resting on his little hands watching every thing. He gazed so hard at the wisemen. All of a sudden, this very still wiseman looked right into Chris's face and winked at him. Well, Chris didn't know what to think about a wiseman winking at him. That was not in any Christmas story he'd ever been told. And he said, "Grandma, that wiseman! He winked at me!" And those around us smiled. . . and I believe the wiseman . . . who was indeed wise that evening. . . took joy in making this little boy happy in the cold of that Christmastide evening.

And it came to pass, as the angels were gone away from them into heaven, the shepherds said one to another. . . Luke 2:15 . . .

. . . Christmas 1995
. . . . the 17th of December

    Christmas has taken hold once more. . . and people (including myself now and again) scurry around in pursuit of "the Christmas spirit." Often one need only be still and it is apt to settle in around him.

    Today I packed a gift to send to a friend who was once a six or seven or eight-year old little girl as was I. I packed a shoebox filled with fruit, nuts, and Christmas candy. I tucked two one-dollar bills in an envelope for Christmas shopping money. . . and a wish list with a place for three Christmas wishes. . . and one of those wishes filled. Not because she needs fruit. . . or nuts. . . or Christmas candies. . . or money to shop with. . . or to ask for three wishes under the tree. . . but just because that was the way it was. . . when she and I were six or seven or eight years old coming to a tree on Christmas morning along with many other little ones who came up in a children's home together . . . who had spent their two dollars on someone else and learned the precious gift of sharing and the specialness of small gifts. She will understand when she opens the gift. . . as no one else could who was not there. Even then the Christ Child was in our hearts for we were taught that that is what Christmas is all about.

    Nowadays, one is apt to trip and fall over gifts that line a room. . . there are so many. Yet I like to

*think it's still about the precious gift of family . . .
friendship . . . and the remembrance of that other gift of
the Christ Child.*

*I think back to a cold and sleeting night back in
November when my car malfunctioned on a busy
parkway. . . and a young couple stopped and "got me
home." We came to know one another a bit in those few
minutes and as I asked for an address to drop a note later
. . . they said "just wish us a safe trip across country for
Thanksgiving. . . that will be enough." I said, "I'll wish
you a guardian angel" and "if you are safe you'll know
the angel was with you."*

*I think of friends who have understood when
standing up for principle caused drifting away from
things that have been important. I think perhaps of
friends whose pathways no longer cross mine because of
those things. . . but now and then God places each of us in
a place where we find one another. . . when neither of us
might normally be there. He places us in one another's
midst. And I think of the friends who won't let you go. . .
because they care. . . telephone calls that make the
difference. I think of friends, too, who perhaps aren't sure
how to say "I care."*

*For reasons not yet settled in my heart I resigned
my worship position this year. . . and feel a bit of a hole. . .
but continue to remember candle lightings. . . choral*

music. . . faith friends. . . and pastors who have been my mentors and have let me spread my wings . . . and fly free . . . to reach another's life.

It is a couple of days later now and I think of a Christmas kindness this morning. . . a lost glove retrieved by another traveler who raced along her way to hand it to me. . . and we wished one another Merry Christmas. . . the kind of Christmas kindness that can find its way into any day. I remember one cold morning offering my gloves to a homeless woman who had none. . . and she smiled and said, "I'll be o.k., but thank you." And I walked along with warm hands and hoped she'd be warm enough, too.

I've enjoyed these evenings when I see my little neighbor girl running over to ring my doorbell as soon as she sees me come in from work . . . sparkling eyes. . . a little smile and often a gift she's made for me. A child! I think, too, of little "Daisy". . . my 3-4 year old friend. . . who likes to come and take me to see Santa . . . or vice versa. I think of her mother too who is like a daughter to me. I think of those who have mothered _me_ over these years along with their own.

As at each Christmas I think of friendships that have lasted half a life-time and beyond. . . some going back home for the holidays. . . north and south. I think of a friend whose son may be destined for Bosnia. . . she's my "haven" and she must be his right now.

Those I work with go to their homes and I to mine after the labors that help provide for home, hearth and Christmas joy. I am grateful to an employer of almost 18 years who has been family and friend to me.

I think, not lastly, but way up at the top of my list, of my children and their children. . . who, as all of us, experience their ups and downs and who get up and try again. They are my extensions and so I feel their joy and their concerns. . . and wish them far horizons to find their dreams. They are beautiful. I see in my mind's eye, too, Maggie and Katie, my cat companions who find warm blankets or the lap of a porcelain doll to make themselves comfortable in these wintry days. I think of two friends who shared Christmas with me and we sang together from a book long about midnight about twelve Christmas cats . . . over and over and over.

I think too of a friend who gifted me with "Dove soap" because I said, "let's get back to basics."

My heart goes out to those who have lost loved ones this year or have otherwise been saddened. . . my merry heart goes out to those who are fortunately joyful and well blessed.

I think of the Christ Child. . . and all my
blessings and I wish you a blessed Christmas. . . with love.

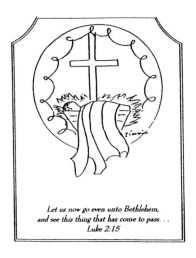

Let us now go even unto Bethlehem,
and see this thing that has come to pass. . .
Luke 2:15

. . . Christmas 1996
Saturday. . . the 21st of December

Christmas comes on quickly now! I send you my prayer for peace in your hearts and love <u>for</u> those around you. . . love <u>from</u> those around you. Christmas brings with it sweet joys. . . tender feelings . . . sometimes a gracious spirit. . . sometimes in other moments. . . sadness.

A friend died yesterday after a short devastating illness. . . and under a cloud of sadness. . . and yet with a given peace. And I wonder why is Death the dramatic statement that calls forth feelings not expressed in time. . . why the roses so late? I'm inclined to think that tho' my friend longed to wait to celebrate one more time the birth of her Lord. . . that He wanted her sooner to join His Christmas angels . . . that His gentle spirit felt she'd had enough.

A little girl sent me gifts by her Mom last Sunday. . . tied by her 5-year old little fingers and picked by her generous little spirit just for me.

Friends came by last night to share my Christmas tree and the tradition of being together as friends for so many years. Others will come tomorrow before they begin their journey north for Christmas. Another long friendship.

Today's moment was a trip to the "Christmas Attic" in Old Towne with my older son, Ronnie, to pick out a figure for his nativity. It is a joyful annual "sojourn" for us. It seems no time since we sat at the kitchen table and he and his brother Jon . . . so small then. . . helped me to hand paint wooden ornaments which still hang in special places on my tree. And there were our gingerbread men, too!

Christmas Eve will bring time with them and their little ones. I hope they sit at a kitchen table and paint ornaments too. Sometime and somewhere that evening I'll make sure I'm in a church pew singing those songs that make the heart swell on Christmas Eve. . . and lighting a candle for the Birthday of the Jesus Child. . . to give Him back a spark of His own light. There will be prayers said in the quiet of myself for those who are without their loves this year . . . a wife or husband. . . a daughter. . . a sister. . . a child. . . a friend. . . and prayers for the new babies born and the gain of love and beauty in the lives of their parents. . . prayers for those disappointed over one thing or another. . . for the wrong doers and the right doers. . . and the joyful.

Seems prayers need to travel so far sometimes and yet there is a place where all prayers are gathered. . . and the message is surely sent on its way by the Great Messenger.

I am thankful for a year of fairly good health

. . . one in which I've been given gracious enough to keep me. . . that I have a small, beautiful family to love. . . friends from Hawaii to California to Colorado to Alabama and Georgia and North and South Carolina to Maryland and Virginia. . . Pennsylvania . . . who are constant in spirit. I'm thankful for good energy for the day's tasks. . . and as often as possible for the day's play.

I'm grateful for an early morning call from an organist who gives his whole self to Christmas Eve to honor the Babe and Mama Mary and loves Worship and its many expressions. I thank him for sharing that.

I'm grateful for Christmas and the reminder from the Christ Child that we are loved.

I wish you the love and wonder of Christmas.

And they came with haste, and found
Mary and Joseph and the babe
lying in a manger.
Luke 2:16

...Christmas 1997

Christmas is a time of light... from the very beginning it was so. From the earliest writings of The Bible, we are told that "In the beginning... God saw that the earth was dark ... and He created the light." John tells us that "In the beginning was the word and the word was with God and the word was God ... in Him there was life and that life was The Light." Countless persons write of the light and how it quells the darkness ... how it illumines the soul ... and the difference our spark of light makes to others.

It seems each year when I begin my Christmas letter, there are so many wonderful thoughts whirling around in my head and heart -- thoughts I want to share. Thoughts more than happenings.

The year has brought moments of light amidst darkness. One thinks of Diana... of Mother Teresa. I think, too, of the singer John Denver whose words and music came to me at a time when I needed to hear them ... to feel a kinship with the world about me... a kinship with myself... and others. I could hear his words and be "in tune" with all that. That voice and that song fell ... hushed ... from the sky as his plane tumbled from the sky ... as Di's goodness folded in the crumpled automobile on a Paris street... and as Mother Teresa's voice and healing hands were brought to rest at a very old age. I think of friends who have lost their mates... and spend

Christmas more alone this year. . . except for the Christmas light. . . which is fueled by love. The light of these and others will be eternal . . . certainly in the lives of those to whom a difference has been made.

I listened one evening in a music store as a "lullaby to a Christmas Tree" played. It was a soft lullaby asking prayers for the skies and the woods and the creatures who live there. I thought about the goodness of that one to whom it was so important to sing about God's creation . . . to treasure it in the spirit as I do. That night animated characters in the store swayed about to the music of the "lullaby." Another evening the song was gone and the motion seemed without motion. . . the music and the words amiss.

My 7-year old granddaughter, Jesse, asked me recently "where did you get that, Mama?" pointing to a nativity made of Indian figures. I told her and asked her to tell me about the scene. She pointed to the teepee and said "that's the manger, Mama." It takes a child. Her little brother looked on and smiled in wonder. They will travel to Florida for Christmas.

My 12-year old grandchild, Chris, said the other night in the midst of our looking at the newest "label," Tommy Hilfigger, "Grandma, you don't need to buy me any of these clothes. . . you can just get me a puzzle or something like that."

I was at a craft fair recently and noticed a small doll whose hands held between them a string holding a button and I wondered if the small children of the world today understand how much fun there can be in twirling a string with a button suspended from it.

I sat in the middle of the floor wrapping gifts the other night for a child sponsored by the Salvation Army Angel Program. I know not what she looks like . . . only that her name is Stephanie, her age is 9, and her size is 10. And I know that it is the only Christmas she will know. It took me back to my childhood shared with a hundred other children with no parents whose Christmas came from Sunday School classes who drew names to buy for. We could ask for three things. I still have an old Bible. . . the print almost too small to read. . . with the pages marked and remarked in red underlining to learn scripture. . . the cover in bad repair. . . and my name misspelled on the front. . . but it was a gift I asked for and one that I got and my heart was happy. It may have been the only gift apart from a shoebox filled with candies and tangerines and the like. It was enough. I could imagine as I wrapped for Stephanie how those Bible Class "angels" must have felt wrapping for us.

I received a note in the mail not long ago from a girl I'd grown up with and not seen for more than 40 years. She remembered. And I received an invitation from the children's home to have an engraved brick placed in my name among others in the Friendship Walk at the

Home where we often gathered for watermelon cuttings, tacky parties on the 4th of July, summer night games and so on. I asked for one for my friend Jossie too and asked that it be put close to mine since we were best friends.

I had an unexpected encounter at breakfast this morning on the way to work with someone who just remembered that she had worked for a short time with me and she sat down with me for coffee. She had lost her grandfather and was sad. I gave her the beginnings of this writing. . . and it caused her to realize the light that her grandfather had left with her . . . . and that will never be quelled by the darkness that came to him.

I shared an 80th birthday celebration for a friend and all her myriad of kids and grandkids and great-grandkids and my heart was warmed by the love between them all. I had scattered moments with close friends and sweet moments with my children.

I had a wonderful vacation in Scandinavia this Fall with a close friend and a former pastor and his wife and other travelers. There too were wonderfully impressive churches where they say "not enough people probably go there either." The people were friendly. . . our Swedish guide was priceless and we had a wonderful driver (also Swedish) whose name was "Sune." We took to calling him "Sooner or Later." Their humor is delightful. The fjords of Norway were majestic with the craggy mountains rising up from them. My appreciation for

God's creation was renewed. . . the beauty that came out of an Ice Age. . . the whole world of creation. . . and on one afternoon as our boat plowed the waters of Norway's fiords and as the mist dampened our faces . . . and I must feel the rain and the sun on my face . . . and a bit of sun peeked out on a far mountainside . . . there were at least four or five rainbows. . . a promise. The stories of trolls in the woods and under the bridges of Norway were fun as were the Viking stories. I am fascinated with that part of the world. Denmark was delightful too with its Tivoli Gardens. . . its Little Mermaid. The harbors in all places were breathtaking. I will go again one day hopefully . . . if only in a dream. The year 2000 will take me to Oberammagau, Germany to see the Passion Play (the story of Christ's final week of agony and resurrection) and to Switzerland, Austria, Liechtenstein, and then to the Holy Land again to see those special places.

My children and grandchildren are doing well. My sons are successful and good people. And goodness is the biggest part of success, I believe. I work hard. . . but work with a fine person who works harder and encourages me when I need it.

I'm trying to get all Christmas fitted in. . . to be with my family to relive Christmas past and dream on days to come. . .to see all the special friends I treasure. . . to nuzzle the kitties who long for me to be home. . . and to get my special prayers said. . . to have time to sing the

Carols of Christmas. . . and to be grateful that we were given a light to fill our spirits and to help us to understand when sometimes we might not.

I wish you all a delightful. . . light filled Christmas. . . and a blessed New Year. My letter is hurried. . . but my wishes are sincere. I think of you all and am glad for each of you in my life.

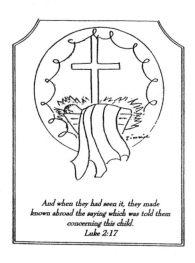

And when they had seen it, they made known abroad the saying which was told them concerning this child.
Luke 2:17

...Christmas 1998

"Moments of Christmas"

"Christmas" comes to each of us in our own personal moments... to each of us at a different time... in a different way... those moments when our spirits become touched by some little thing... tangible... but mostly intangible. Oftentimes it's what we do for a friend... with a friend... or the friend does for or with us. It is in the moment we spend with a friend helping her trim her tree with ornaments clothed in sweet memories... but perhaps glistening now with a tear for want of another time.

It may come as we sit down to an abundant Thanksgiving dinner and call out the blessings we have ... the things we're grateful for... and the small ones at the table say "my family." On the Friday after Thanksgiving, my smallest grandchildren, Jessica (8) and Zachary (5), stayed the day and helped me to decorate for my Christmas moments ... and these became my beginning Christmas moments this year... the Thanksgiving meal and the day that followed. Jesse, so young and yet so wise and so sweet and beautiful helped her little brother to "learn how" and a bit of magic settled over these little helping hands that placed the blue lights ... the crystal beads... and a candy-striped "praise stick" she brought last year... and of course ornaments that go back to their dad's day. I noticed after they left that *evening that a sleigh rested atop the stable and an angel was holding the reins. My 13-year old Chris is growing up quickly these days and "slapping his face" with Polo Sport and is into every sport that comes along. My two sons are to be proud of. . . they're interesting. . . colorful . . . hardworking and good. I remember when it was their little hands who helped to hang gingerbread men on the tree. . . our Christmas vacation together and the trips to the mall to spend their little Christmas money.*

Christmas may come to us if we ride the carousel with children and your own little ones smile that you will ride too. . . as the music box sounds and the horses go up and down and round and round and little hands hold on tight . . . and the twinkling lights dazzle their minds. Christmas may happen in the early evening before all the stars of night come if we look up to the heavens and see a crescent moon with a single star overhead. . . that is, if we share it with someone else . . . a child who is apt to say "do you think they're talking to one another?" And yes, I do believe they are.

A Christmas moment came to me when I spontaneously stopped by to see my dear friend. . . to share a bit of coffee and "pumpkinbread man." Five hours later I went home. In those five hours "Precious Moments" came to life on table tops showing the wonder of childlikeness and the sweetness of the nativity seen as a child would. . . . Santa took his place of honor on the mantle. A bit of Christmas came to us as friends. . . and a memory for future ones.

Christmas comes to me this evening as I write this and look beyond my evergreen table arrangement to where my tabby cat Katie looks back at me from her beautiful green eyes. . . beautiful even though she is not having a well Christmas. I look at her and her <u>brother</u>, Maggie, and realize that they have given me 13 years of Christmas joy as they take pleasure in the tree, the twinkling lights, the music that is so special at this time and the warm lap of one who loves them.

The evergreen arrangement on the table reminds me that my children love me and I them. . . though time slips through fingers. . . and the heart wants to draw the children back to love them longer. Christmas offers moments that make it possible. I remember another bouquet not long ago from my other son which was a token of his caring.

Christmas comes to me now as I search for words to make a difference. . . as I seek to write "Words to Grow On" for others when I have so much growing to do myself. Yet, when I reach out to find words they have been put there for my heart to know and my pen to write. Christmas comes as our new handbell choir practices its carols for worship on Sunday. . . and I ask your prayers for my E, F and F# notes. I will pray too for the Lord to use my hands and put good spirit in the notes that come.

Christmas came earlier this evening as I put Salvation Army pick-up stickers on a little girl's bike and scooter for some little child to have for Christmas. They belonged to my 11-year old neighbor Katie whose adoptive single Mom died suddenly a few weeks ago . . . too suddenly to say their goodbyes. . . too suddenly for Christmas to come to them this year. . . too suddenly to give Katie my hugs and help dry her tears. But she is in another lap of love and she will remember her Mom at Christmas.

Christmas came in a concert lately . . . "The Very First Christmas" done in a "folk way." Words about Bethlehem. . . Mary. . . Joseph. . . the Baby . . . and the humbleness of it all. You know the story.

Christmas came lately too in a long awaited soft evening rain . . . gentle like the Christ Child. . . bringing the fragrance of life to the drying leaves of Fall. . . reminding us that the Christ Child can bring newness to our lives.

And, of course, Christmas comes in the "Silent Night" and in "Oh, Little Town of Bethlehem" and we remember what it's about. . . not so much about ourselves but the Christ Child in us.

I and mine are mostly fine. . . too busy!!! I was thinking little rhymes today about. . .

"Bells to ring. . . words to tell. . .
no time for ribbon. . . no time for string. . .
but here is my Christmas offering."

The mind is a-whirl. Life is a'hurry. I'm glad for
moments with family. . . friends. . . new experiences and
more.

Wherever and however Christmas comes to you I
hope it settles all around you with love and joy and that
it fills any sad spots with new hope.

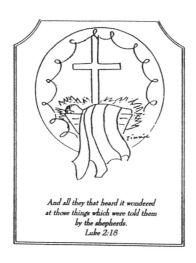

And all they that heard it wondered
at those things which were told them
by the shepherds.
Luke 2:18

. . . Christmas 1999

A merry Christmas to each of you! I hope each of you comes to the end of the year with good memories. . . some prosperity. . . good health. . . and folks to love you.

My year has blessed me in many ways. . . and in times when I felt a need for blessing. . . comfort came from somewhere. . . the love and understanding from a caring heart. . . or through answered prayer.

I watched my children and grandchildren turn another year older. . . and looked upon them with pride. And now and again I watched as I turned older too. Ronnie coached youth football again this year and led his team to championship. He feels good about that . . . not just for the winning but more for the mark he hopes to make on these young lives. His son Chris (now 14) is in high school. . . is growing in statue and in wisdom and is delightful among other people. Jon and his wife Allison recently moved into their "dream house" where their two little ones, Jessica (9) and Zachary (6) seem to be enjoying themselves and are sweet little people.

For the last year I've been privileged to write "Words to Grow On" for the Methodist women in my church. I pull at my heart strings regularly to try to find words worthy to share. They're mostly well received.

One of my "Words" this summer was called "His Name Was Maggie". . . an article about my 14-year old kitty who courageously battled cancer. . . bravely yielded to chemotherapy and was doing so well. . . until a brain tumor took him away. He was my "furperson" and I his "human." My eyes tear up still when I think about him. He left Katie, his little tabby friend, also 14 years old. She grieves over him, and has not yet been able to accept Midge, a young cat who looks almost identical to Maggie but is of a very different spirit. We're working together on love and understanding and social graces. I have made a Christmas vignette for Maggie, all kitties and angel kitties. Hopefully Midge will prove to be a bright spot in Katie's little despair. A copy of my "words" about Maggie follows for some of you knew and loved him too. It is called "His Name Was Maggie." Surely his spirit will light around my Christmas tree where he so loved to be. And I will put a doll beneath the tree to keep him company. . . and Katie too.

I am fresh back from a visit with my childhood friend, Jossie. We shared a bit of early Christmas together. . . put up her tree . . . went to see a performance of a "Living Christmas Tree" which had a choir of 118 people singing from the inside and the heights of three very large trees. The trees were lighted and with Christmas colors that changed with each carol sung. It was magnificent. It brought to mind a Christmas tree in the middle of the lawn at the "Home" where she and I grew up together. It always seemed magical. I came to know again how dear she is to me and how much those years together and those since mean to me. I'm proud that all who know her love her.

I'm still a part of the bell choir at church and we will ring on Sunday morning and at our Christmas concert that night. It's a beautiful challenge and good therapy. We're still in our early stages, but are getting better.

Christmas will offer time with my family and friends. . . and I wish that part of that could be spent with you.

I hope for a trip to Switzerland, Austria, Germany, Liechtenstein and The Holy Land in September of the New Year, but it remains to be seen. Things like Maggie's illness impacted on other things. Yet Maggie was a dear part of me. . . and his life was important too and my heart dictated what I should do for him. Life will go on. . . if sadly at times and surely God will watch over Maggie. . . for he is His creation.

Christmas is rushing me. . . or I it. . . and so my letter may have a different tone than in the past. In the place of that other spirit. . . I offer you a copy of my "Words to Grow On" for the New Year and wish you all good things as you move into that time. I think of you and wish you all God's best.

"His Name Was Maggie"
from "Words to Grow On"
September 1999

One must write about what one knows. . . and one most often grows from life experiences . . . so I write today about what I have known the most since I wrote you last . . . and from what I've felt the most growth. His name was Maggie. . . .

I will take long walks in the days to come and try to commune with our Creator and the Creator of the small things that walk upon the earth. I will search for the spirit of Him and of one called Maggie . . . who came to be in my midst long years ago. . . just a kitten with patch eyes. . . and ears too big and a tail too long for his body.

In our midst we often find extra reason to love . . . a source of growth. We can learn from these creatures of God . . . as they show us warmth. . . understanding. . . patience to wait. . . and humor. Though they were created lower than ourselves. . . and though we were given dominion over them. . . we can learn from them. We accept their devotion . . . we cherish their gladness to see us. . . we may stand amazed at their ways of communication. . . silent communication. We may be thankful for their unconditional acceptance and love for us and their greetings at the door or through a snow-laden window make our hearts glad. They entertain us as they crouch low with ears pricked high . . . looking at a bird up in its nest . . . crouching, though, in a spot smaller than they. . . believing they cannot be seen . . . or as they try to catch a snowflake on the other side of the window. They watch a leaf drift down from a branch and want it for their own. They see tiny little things that we cannot see. They leap to high places . . . as did their ancestral cats. . . and seclude themselves in the low. They play games . . . and are often smarter than we. They respond to us with purrs and twirling tails and eyes that gaze into our hearts.

They teach us courage. . . they don't complain. They teach us independence and self reliance . . . yet we cause them to depend upon us. We gain strength from them. . . and weep in their distress. One day we find ourselves with empty laps that were warm before . . . a place on our pillow once alive with little kitty breaths . . . tickling whiskers. . . the gentle tap of a paw that says "let me come rest there too." All is silent now . . . . We yearn to fill the water bowl and the food tray. . . to see the scurrying of little cat feet. And our hearts become empty for the place they used to fill. They teach us that burden is not really burden . . . that inconvenience is only minor . . . that to stop for them . . . to stroke them gently . . . does not slow us down but rather brings a moment of peace. It paces us. It is no real effort to sweep up the few crumbs that they strew. . . or the bits of litter that they kick from their boxes. . . perhaps the worst thing one of these little ones may do is nibble the baby's breath from a flower *arrangement. . . pull the telephone from its cradle. We give back in small measure.*

Maggie taught me courage throughout his surgery. . . and weeks of chemotherapy. . . days when we developed an even deeper companionship. He snuggled beneath my chin as I gave him comfort in a place in my garden on a July morning where I rocked him in his little quilt. . . talked to him. . . prayed over him. . . shed many tears . . . and where he could hear the birds sing and feel the sunshine . . . . He went to sleep that next day of a tumor that grew quietly in his brain unknown to any of us. . . even as he was healing. He gave me comfort in times when I, too, needed healing. So I shall walk these next days. . . weeks and months. . . as Maggie did in his last days . . . too courageous to give up. . . wanting to go on. He has taught me courage, gentleness, great love, understanding, the value of life and that giving our best is never too much. . . that becoming involved makes love grow. . . and true caring insists on involvement. He came to be in my midst. . . and I was blessed. . . and I am humbled at his passing. But, you know. . . last evening I was sure I felt him jump up on the bed. . . yet I looked and saw him not. I share this with you in love. . . knowing that if you've had such a friend. . . you'll understand. I learned too that in my midst was a friend to help get me through.

Words to Grow On for The New Year

"A Star to Guide Us"

IT IS EPIPHANY... and I can think of no better way to celebrate the New Millennium than to be guided by The Star of Bethlehem... as were the Wisemen ... to find the Christ Child anew and to keep That Star ... That Light... That Christ to show us the way. Remembering that it began a long, long time ago.

THEY SAY "RING OUT THE OLD... RING IN THE NEW!" Yet, like the Christmas Wreath... and like Christmas and Easter... like The Birth... The Crucifixion... The Resurrection.... Indeed, like The Life of Christ... The Old and The New... The Beginning and the End and likewise The End and The Beginning — aren't they really a part of the same? Can there be one without the other? And wasn't there newness on either end of Christ's life? And at each beginning and ending of nature... isn't there?

AND SO I SAY, "Ring not out the Old, but ring for the Old... for how can we leave its beauty behind ... its joys... its friendships... its chances for a better tomorrow... its times of dreaming... of building... its seasons of youth... of springtime and blossoming... its seasons of settling in... its autumn... its seasons in the sun... coming to know oneself and others... its time for healing? How can we forget the excitement along the way

. . . the sweetness of memories which help our hearts to go on beating. . . our spirits to soar. . . our minds to grow, building all that has been into all that is to be?

AND I SAY ALSO, "Bring this with you as preparation for the new. . . something to pass on to those who come behind. . . ."

BUT THEN RING WITH ALL YOUR HEARTS for the Hope with which Christ refreshes each day as a gift to us . . . the gift that was lent us at Christmastime tied with the love and comfort He has promised us if we acknowledge Him in all our ways and look to Him to direct our paths in all time to come.

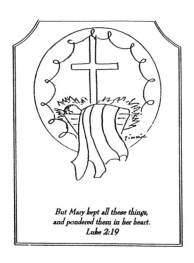

But Mary kept all these things,
and pondered them in her heart.
Luke 2:19

. . . Christmas 2000

It's going on Christmas now. . .
and I think back to these last days . . .
weeks and months since I last shared
Christmas with you.

On Labor Day of this year I put on my walking
shoes and picked up my bags . . . amidst many things
happening. . . and flew off to Europe and The Holy Land
for two weeks. I will copy my earlier thoughts of my trip
below rather than try to recreate them at this very busy
time . . . for they were fresher right after the trip than
they can be in the midst of late night sitting in the floor
wrapping gifts and tying ribbons. . . running them to the
post office . . . making sure to attend bell choir practices so
that I don't ring out of tune on Sundays and especially
on Christmas Eve when one would want to give her best
in celebration. . . and trying to make sure no one is
forgotten in the remembrance of Christmas. . . trying to
put aside things that sting the heart at times. . . trying to
bring in things that warm one's spirit. . . trying to do
something good for someone else who has less. . . trying to
remember Christmas for what it is intended to be rather
than what we earthlings sometimes make it . . . trying to
remember in the heart to do unto others as we would have
them to do. . . not necessarily as they do. Trying to be
generous of heart. . . spirit and purse. I am glad to know
in my heart that there are little boys and girls in a home
far away who each have a teddy bear. . . a homemade

quilt and a Bible to call their very own . . . to nurture them. . . to make them warm and to give them a symbol of something to love and hold onto.

Most of the year was similar to years past. . . busy days. . . long days and short nights. . . celebrations with friends and family here and there . . . thoughts of retirement one day. . . but not today . . . many good things for which to be grateful. . . some not so good from which to learn. . . a chance to write "Words to Grow On" for the United Methodist Women in my church and others who are interested in my effort at saying something that will perhaps cause one to grow. . . to laugh. . . maybe shed a tear. . . to feel a sense of connection. . . something to relate to. . . and I will do this yet a third year in 2001 and I am honored.

My sons continue to wear a bit of a cloud since their father's tragic death in July. Prayerfully, this Christmastime. . . though it will cause the heart to feel someone and some things missing. . . it will also cause the heart to remember days that were good . . . will bring them some peace . . . and with the New Year will come healing for them. We all know how we feel the pain of our children.

In spite of their sadness they continue to do well in their lives . . . as their own persons. . . as parents and family. . . and as helpers in the world. Their children in turn are holding their own.

My older son coached Chantilly (Virginia) youth league football yet another year and yet another year led them to their regional winnings. He is looked upon with great respect by his team players and their parents for what he teaches the boys not just about winning but how they go about it. His son Chris is 15 going on 16 now and in high school playing football and wrestling there. A fine boy indeed!

My younger son Jon prospers too in different ways . . . serves well as the service director of an Acura dealership, where he endeavors to teach those in his charge good work ethic and determination and the art of energy. He is a good father and husband and busily watches his son Zachary at age 7 out on the football field butting helmets with the other kids. Zachary got his first little trophy this year and is happy about it. My daughter-in-law Allison taught the team cheerleaders who seemed to be the best in the league and were capable of doing "half-time" shows with great finesse. Jessica, Zachary's older sister, is one of those, and a young girl of beauty and tenderness. . . and one who has her own ideas about many, many things.

My thoughts go out to so many . . . to friends and others whose health has failed them lately and who otherwise have known misfortune. . . to those who have had reasons for joy. My thoughts and prayers travel along with those who will be celebrating the holidays *elsewhere. I wish you safe travel and memories in the making.*

The new kitty in the house. . . Midge. . . is making her own way and is finding herself comfortable there. She's different from my Maggie whom I lost last year. . . but has her own way that is loving. . . teasing. . . and reserves a bit of her own dignity for herself. She makes her own decisions about when what happens to her. Katie. . . my little going-on-16 tabby kitty. . . is slower these days . . . but sweet . . . and lives in her "retirement home" under the powder room vanity. She's taken to wanting her water out of the bathroom sink. . . and so of course Midge does too. I still must put up my tree, I believe, for they will want it up to look at the lights and perhaps find a shiny ornament to call their own, and they will tell me so, too, as they tell me so many other things. I may have to put Katie a tree of her own in the powder room. . . so that she realizes that Christmas is for her too.

As I share with you now a writing I did after my trip. . . I will also wish you a warm and tender Christmas. . . filled with joy and love for someone else. Thank you to my family and friends for loving me. . . and understanding me when I cannot be all that I might be. My words are called "Jerusalem Light" which is appropriate. . . though I might prefer to think of the "Bethlehem Light" at least right now.

"Jerusalem Light"

It is said that one comes to know Jerusalem and the Holy Land best through one's senses -- touch, smell, sound, feeling, and knowing the light that is somehow different there.

It was the Sabbath. . . and it was Galilee. Our group would soon be setting out on a boat across the Sea of Galilee. . . a boat not wholly unlike one in which Jesus would have spent time.

But for Now, the early morning light from beyond that sea awoke me, and I went to my window and opened it . . . to feel the sea air and to watch for the sunrise and to fill my spirit for this day that would take us to the Mount of Beatitudes where I would be privileged to read those words. . . where my heart would swell at reading His Words. . . His Beatitudes . . . in a place where He had also spoken them.

But for Now, I watched the Eastern Sky unfold her morning and later I would share with the group this encounter with the Galilean sunrise and with the Lord:

"We are in a special place. . . here on this mount . . . here above the Sea of Galilee . . . another of those places where Jesus walked. I don't know how many of you looked out to watch the sunrise this morning. . . but I did. It peeked over the hill beyond this lake sending out its

*burst of pink rays as if on an Easter morning. I stood at
my window. . . turning away now and then to prepare for
the day. . . but still watching as the scene changed. . .
rapidly and beautifully. At one point I looked over my
shoulder to see that the gentle layers of morning cloud
before the bright sun formed a perfect Jerusalem cross. . .
the cross superimposed on the rising sun. . . the sun
shining forth from four corners and at the center. I was
stilled in my tracks and could only say, 'My Lord, can
this be happening to me?'*

*"A friend from another place wondered with me
at breakfast what each of us will take home with us from
this trip. Look about you, gather your images, place
yourself in this place of Christ, feel the air, perhaps
remember the quiet sounds of the sea. . . the gentle rocking
of the boat earlier today. . . the murmurings of the leaves
on these trees. . . close your eyes and capture these
beatitudes in your spirit for they teach us how to be like
Christ. He told us in simple words the kind of person He
was and the blessings attached to our emulating Him.
You may never be the same.*

> *'And seeing the multitudes, He went up into a
> mountain: and when he was set, his disciples came
> unto Him: And he opened his mouth, and taught
> them saying:*
>
> *Blessed are the poor in spirit: for theirs is the kingdom
> of heaven.*

Blessed are they that mourn: for they shall be
comforted.
Blessed are the meek: for they shall inherit the earth.
Blessed are they which do hunger and thirst after
righteousness: for they shall be filled.
Blessed are the merciful: for they shall obtain mercy.
Blessed are the pure in heart: for they shall see God.
Blessed are the peacemakers: for they shall be called the
children of God.
Blessed are they which are persecuted for righteousness'
sake: for theirs is the kingdom of heaven.
Blessed are ye, when men shall revile you and persecute
you and shall say all manner of evil against
you falsely, for my sake.
Rejoice, and be exceeding glad: for great is your
reward in heaven: for so persecuted they the
prophets which were before you.'"

Someone standing close by said "I didn't realize
what a difference this [being in this place] makes." And
someone said at supper, "Sally saw the Jerusalem cross
also." To the waiting heart. . . there cometh.

And in the night sky over the Galilean Sea rose
the moon and came the stars shimmering on the Sea
water just as they must have for Him so long ago. And I
didn't want to go to sleep so that I might hang on to all
this.

Light Manifests Itself [Himself] in countless
ways:

Before we came to The Holy Land, we visited Austria and other places in Europe where we saw the sun lay itself on the tops of high mountains and move across the deep valleys which often hide in shadow and the late day sun put the earth to rest as we concluded our day's journeys.

We visited a village church just a walk away from our hotel where a cemetery lay protected in its backyard . . . family plot by family plot with live flowers growing atop each and where someone said "If you find this lovely now. . . I urge you to come back at evening when the candles on the graves are lit. You'll find the lights to be very special." And I and a few others did. . . and found the candlelight speaking in the night for those resting there. . . and I looked up to the church tower to see that yet a bit of light was in the sky. . . that very, very dark blue that one sometimes sees.

In Jerusalem we visited the Holocaust Museum dedicated to the Jewish children who perished in that very ungodly circumstance. One part of the museum housed a room masked in darkness, except for a dimly lit walkway with a handrail and in the black space about us were suspended tiny white lights. . . and a voice called out continuously the names of children lost -- with only those small white lights and the sound of the voice breaking the dark -- in an effort to hang on to those children -- to never forget them.

We saw the Light in the hearts of our Jewish guide and our Palestinian driver who taught us and shepherded us about each day. They were friends and played on the humor of one another and respected the concerns of one another and showed us that there is hope for their land.

We saw Light in the heart of one young person of fame who moved quietly among us and whose eyes shone sincerity as his hand reached out to help someone to climb steps or move across rocky places.

In most churches which we visited we saw lights -- lights lit in the name of the Lord and of loved ones.

We saw a Morning Light warming the Garden Tomb and a special light around our group as we communed together.

We saw Light in the eyes of those who came in throngs to see these places. . . to feel these places. . . to kneel at them. . . and to walk in that special light where Christ walked and does walk.

. . . continues

As we traveled to the airport at 3:00 o'clock in the morning of our last day we listened to strains of an old, old song that spoke of Jerusalem... the hosannas that people sang to the Lord... the eternal hosannas. And as we listened we remembered... and will long remember.

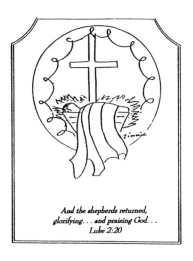

And the shepherds returned,
glorifying... and praising God...
Luke 2:20

. . . Christmas 2001

As I look towards Christmas this year. . . I must also look back at the year just past . . . as time past is part of time present and builds for time to come.

My heart smiles with pride on my sons and their accomplishments this year . . . accomplishments brought on by their sense of moral character and determination. My heart cries at the loss of loved ones this year and the illness of others. My heart is satisfied that there has been enough to make me comfortable . . . and that I am given inner strength to handle things I must. My heart rests . . . is warm . . . and feels safe that the light of Christ shines upon me to show me the way.

I remember special moments of course from last Christmas . . . one of them being my granddaughter, Jesse, sitting at a small desk, studying with a delightful mind my Boyd's Bear Nativity. . . just as it says a "nativity of bears" playacting out the Christmas story. I had the pieces organized in the way that I think of Christmas. I watched her as she moved pieces from here to there in the way that she thinks about Christmas being. And I wonder to myself. . . just how different are the ways in which we see Christmas. . . certainly the heart of it is love. I have seen it in the eyes of my children and now their children and those others in my life whom I have come to care about.

A Child's Prayer

*I include the following prayer as part of this
Christmas greeting because I believe there is purity in the
heart of a child. . . just as there was certain purity in the
heart of That Original Christmas Child. It was written
by my son, Ronnie. There are things of our children that
we tuck away in special places . . . others in our hearts. . .
little bits and pieces of paper that get lost along the way
that were so precious to us . . . that we'd never want them
to get lost. . . and yet, they do. I have another poem
somewhere . . . written for me by my son Jon . . . about his
little hands and "see how they grow." And they have . . .
into strong and able hands.*

*The child's prayer that follows has survived time
and I share it with you. It's about the heart of our family
. . . and surely families must continue to hold on to one
another . . . care for. . . and pray for one another each
day.*

"Heavenly Lord, hear my prayer,
Watch over us,
Through the Midnight air;
Bless my Mom, for she is soft;
And bless my Dad, for he is strong.
Watch over them the whole day long;
Watch over me, and my brother, too,
For we are tired from the day so long,
And take care of us while our parents are gone.
. . . A-men."
Ronnie Goings

Christmas Postscript

As I close this greeting. . . I'm reminded that my Christmas tree has called to me strongly one more year and helped me to understand that it and its twinkling lights and shiny ornaments are so important to Christmas. . . and yes, I must put the tree up and did. . . long about 2:00 o'clock in the morning a few nights ago

. . .

not long before the morning light. . . and in time for the celebration of The True Light.

I wish you that Light always.

Zimmie

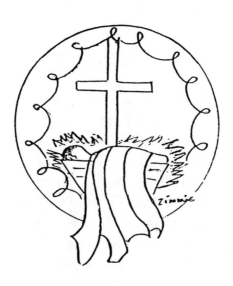

Your Christmas Memories

Your Christmas Memories . . . continued

Your Christmas Memories . . . continued

Your Christmas Memories . . . continued

Your Christmas Memories . . . continued

Your Christmas Memories . . . continued

Your Christmas Memories . . . continued

Your Christmas Memories . . . continued

Your Christmas Memories . . . continued

Your Christmas Memories . . . continued

Your Christmas Memories . . . continued